Making Difficult Words Easy

Code Reader Books provide codes with "sound keys" to help read difficult words. For example, a word that may be difficult to read is "unicorn," so it might be followed by a code like this: unicorn *(YOO-nih-korn)*. By providing codes with phonetic sound keys, Code Reader Books make reading easier and more enjoyable.

Examples of Code Reader™ Keys

Long a sound (as in make):
a *(with a silent e)* or **ay**
Examples: able *(AY-bul)*; break *(brake)*

Short i sound (as in sit): **i** or **ih**
Examples: myth *(mith)*; mission *(MIH-shun)*

Long i sound (as in by):
i *(with a silent e)* or **y**
Examples: might *(mite)*; bicycle *(BY-sih-kul)*

Keys for the long o sound (as in hope):
o *(with a silent e)* or **oh**
Examples: molten *(MOLE-ten)*; ocean *(OH-shen)*

Codes use dashes between syllables *(SIH-luh-buls)*, and stressed syllables have capital letters.

To see more Code Reader sound keys, see page 43.

Killer Bees and Hornets

TREASURE BAY

Killer Bees and Hornets
A Code Reader™ Book
Green Series

This book, along with with images and text, is published
under license from The Creative Company. Originally published as
Killer Bees and Asian Giant Hornets © 2024 Black Rabbit Books

Additions and revisions to text in this
licensed edition: Copyright © 2025 Treasure Bay, Inc.
Additional images provided by iStock

All rights reserved.

Reading Consultant: Jennifer L. VanSlander, Ph.D., Asst. Professor
of Educational Leadership, Columbus State University

Code Reader™ is a trademark of Treasure Bay, Inc.

Patent Pending.
Code Reader books are designed using an innovative system of methods
to create and include phonetic codes to enhance the readability of text.
Reserved rights include any patent rights.

Published by
Treasure Bay, Inc.
PO Box 519
Roseville, CA 95661 USA

Printed in China

Library of Congress Control Number: 2024944966

ISBN: 978-1-60115-726-3

Visit us online at:
CodeReader.org

PR-1-25

CHAPTER 1	Invaders *(in-VAY-durz)* 2
CHAPTER 2	Killer Bee Takeover *(TAKE-oh-vur)* .. 4
CHAPTER 3	Size and Features 8
CHAPTER 4	Killer Bees: Where They Live 12
CHAPTER 5	Life Cycle *(SY-kul)* 14
CHAPTER 6	Watch Out for Killer Bees! 18
CHAPTER 7	Killer Hornets 22
CHAPTER 8	Size and Features *(FEE-churz)* 26
CHAPTER 9	Where They Live and What They Eat 34
CHAPTER 10	Watch Out for Hornets! 38
	Glossary 42
	Sound Keys for Codes 43
	Questions to Think About 44

CHAPTER 1

(in-VAY-durz)

Invasive *(in-VAY-siv)* insects are an increasing danger *(DANE-jur)* to people. These are insects that have somehow spread from their original *(or-RIH-jih-nul)* habitats to a new part of the world. The spread of invasive insects is usually *(YOO-zhoo-uh-lee)* due to something humans have done. Two of the scariest invasive insects are killer bees and giant *(JY-ent)* hornets.

These frightening insects are not just dangerous to humans. They are also a growing danger to honeybees *(HUN-nee-BEEZ)*.

Honeybees are very important for much of the food we eat. They pollinate *(POL-lih-nate)* about 75 percent of the fruit *(froot)*, nuts, and vegetables *(VEJ-tuh-bulz)* grown in the United *(yoo-NY-ted)* States. Without bees, much of the food we eat could not be grown. But honeybees are being killed and their hives taken over by killer bees and giant hornets.

CHAPTER 2

Killer Bee

(TAKE-oh-ver)

A honeybee hive buzzes. Inside, the bees feed their young and make honey. Outside, killer bees approach. They need a need place to live. And the honeybee hive will make a great spot. The queen killer bee and a few of its workers crawl inside. The takeover *(TAKE-oh-ver)* has begun *(bee-GUN)*.

5

Attack!

The killer bees find the honeybee queen. They kill it. The killer bee queen then takes over the hive. It begins laying eggs. Meanwhile, the workers fight off attacking honeybees. The nest will soon be filled with killer bees.

Killer bees don't just kill honeybees. They can kill other animals, even people *(PEE-pul)*!

CHAPTER 3

Size and FEATURES

HEAD

ANTENNAE
(an-TEN-nee)

LEGS

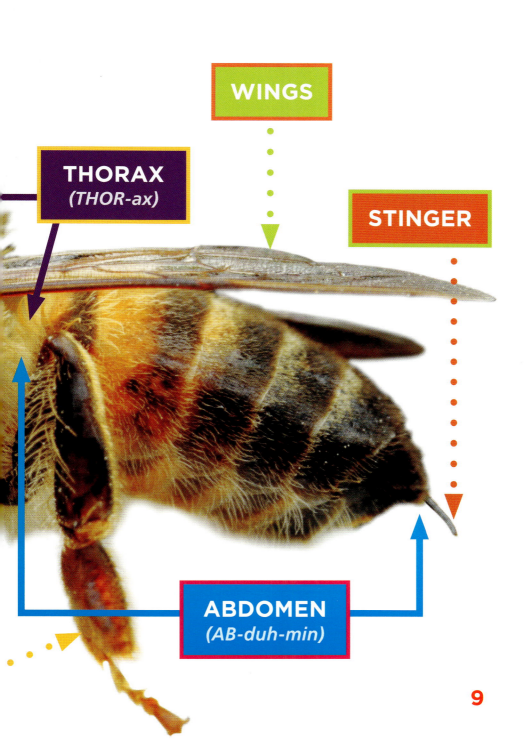

Killer bees do not have more venom *(VEN-um)* than other bees. But large groups of killer bees attack at once *(wuns)*. They will also chase people or animals farther than other bees.

Serious Stingers

These fierce *(FEERes)* bees earned their name. They will stop at nothing *(NUH-thing)* to protect their hives from other animals. They sting with venom *(VEN-um)*. Only females *(FEE-mails)* have stingers. The stingers grow from the same body parts that lay eggs. Stingers have small hooks on them. The hooks get stuck in animals and people. After the bees sting, the stingers are ripped from their bodies. The bees die soon after.

CHAPTER 4

Killer Bees:

Killer bees first appeared *(uh-PEERD)* in Brazil *(brah-ZIL)* in the 1950s. Scientists *(SY-en-tists)* there were working with African *(AF-rih-can)* and European *(yur-roh-PEE-an)* honeybees. They wanted to create *(kree-ATE)* bees that could make more honey and handle hotter temperatures *(TEM-pur-uh-churz)*. The scientists accidentally created a new aggressive *(uh-GRES-siv)* type of bee. Then some of those bees escaped. They began to spread and grow. These bees are also called Africanized *(AF-rih-can-nize-d)* honeybees.

Today, killer bees live all across South and Central America. They have also now spread to the southern part of the United States.

Killer bee colonies *(KOL-uh-neez)* live in hives. They often build *(bild)* their hives in trees. • • • ▶ They also take over hives from honeybees.

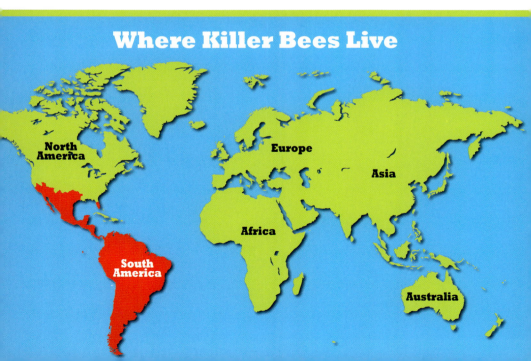

Where Killer Bees Live

CHAPTER 5

LIFE CYCLE
(SY-cul)

Each killer bee colony *(KOL-uh-nee)* has a queen. The queen lays all of the eggs for the colony. The young hatch as larvae *(LAR-vee)*. Worker bees care for the larvae and the queen. Killer bees grow from egg to adult *(uh-DULT)* in about 21 days.

From Egg to ADULT

EGG

Killer bee queens can lay up to 1,500 eggs a day. A queen lays one egg in each cell.

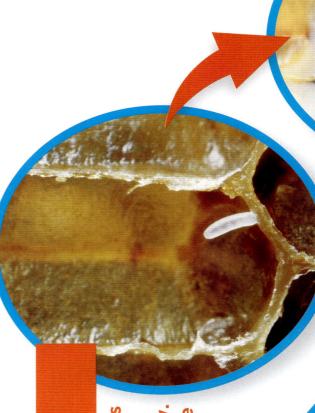

LARVA *(LAR-vuh)*
Workers feed the larva.

PUPA *(PYOO-puh)*
The pupa looks like a pale adult bee.

ADULT
Adults that become queens do nothing but lay eggs. Workers care for the young and find food.

17

CHAPTER 6

for Killer Bees!

Killer bees might look like regular *(REG-yoo-lar)* honeybees, but they don't act like them. Killer bees get angry when people get too close. Thousands of killer bees pour out of the nest. They chase and swarm people. They sting a person's eyes, mouth, and nose. Too much venom can be deadly *(DED-lee)*. It causes organ *(OR-gen)* failure, which can lead to death. These dangerous *(DANE-jer-us)* bugs give regular honeybees a bad name.

Both honeybees and killer bees produce honey we can eat. Beekeepers wear suits *(soots)* that protect them from the bees.

BY THE NUMBERS

FLYING SPEED — **12 to 15 MILES PER HOUR**

ABOUT 1,000
NUMBER OF KILLER BEE STINGS NEEDED TO KILL AN ADULT HUMAN

50 DAYS
average *(AV-ur-ej)* life span of worker killer bees

0.25 MILE
distance *(DIS-tens)* killer bees will chase people

1990
Africanized *(AF-rih-can-nize-d)* bees came to Texas in this year

CHAPTER 7

Killer

A colony *(KOL-uh-nee)* of honeybees works inside its hive. Suddenly, a buzzing sound comes from outside. An Asian *(AY-zhen)* giant *(JY-ent)* hornet crawls into the hive. The hornet scout marks the nest with a scent *(sent)*. Then it waits.

Attack!

More giant hornets follow the scent to the hive. They swarm the honeybees, stinging and biting them. Soon, the hornets kill all the honeybees. They chew up the bees. They bring the mashed-up bees to their nest to feed their young.

Hornets are a type of wasp *(wahsp)*.

CHAPTER 8

Size and
(FEE-churz)

No other hornet on Earth matches up to the Asian giant hornet's size. It is the world's biggest hornet. At up to two inches long, these hornets rule the sky. Two sets of gray wings help them speed after prey *(pray)*.

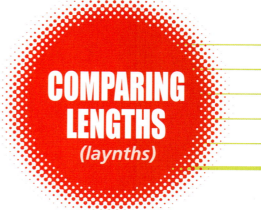

COMPARING LENGTHS
(laynths)

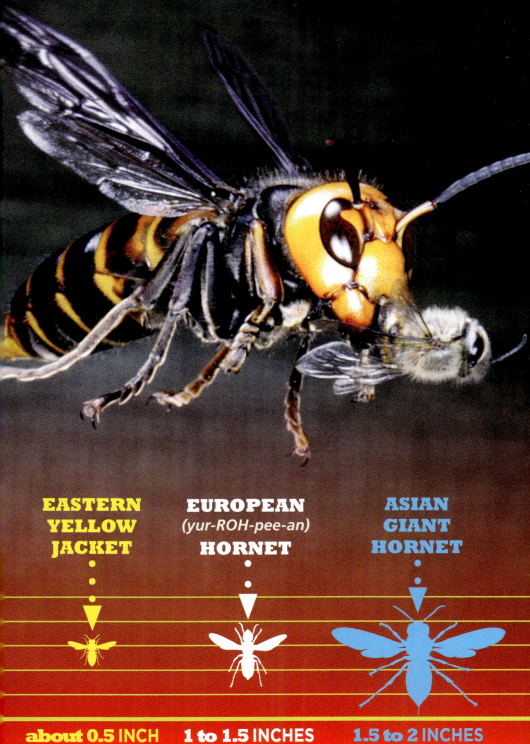

Asian giant hornets have strong mouthparts. They use them to bite and kill their prey.

Bug Body

Asian giant hornets have six legs and three body parts. The head is yellowish orange. The thorax is brown. The abdomen *(AB-duh-min)* has bands of yellow and black.

These bugs have compound eyes. Each eye has many tiny lenses *(LEN-zez)*. The lenses can see in many directions at once. Two antennae *(an-TEN-nee)* stick out from the head. They help the hornets smell and feel.

Vicious *(VIH-shus)* Venom

An Asian giant hornet stings with venom. The poison kills quickly. The hornet's stinger is 0.25 inches long. Only females have stingers. The stinger is connected to the part of the body that lays eggs. Asian giant hornets have smooth stingers. Their stingers don't get stuck in prey. They can sting again and again.

Japanese *(jap-puh-NEEZ)* honeybees protect their hives by swarming Asian giant hornet scouts. The honeybees then move back and forth quickly. This movement *(MOOV-ment)* makes a lot of heat. The bees cook the hornet to death. It can't bring more hornets to the hive.

PARTS OF AN ASIAN GIANT HORNET

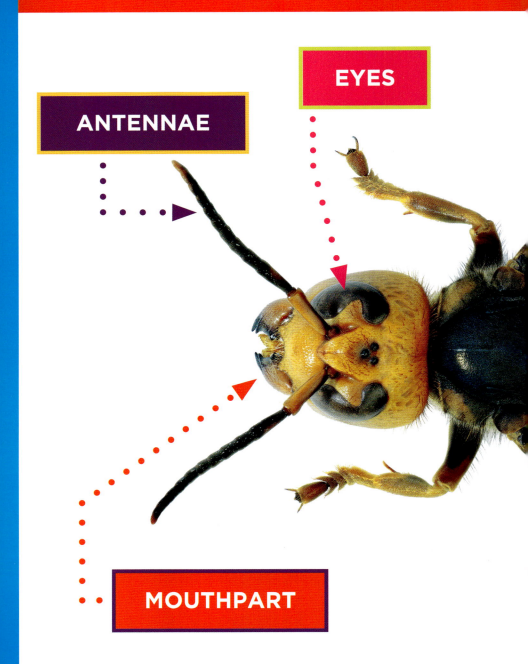

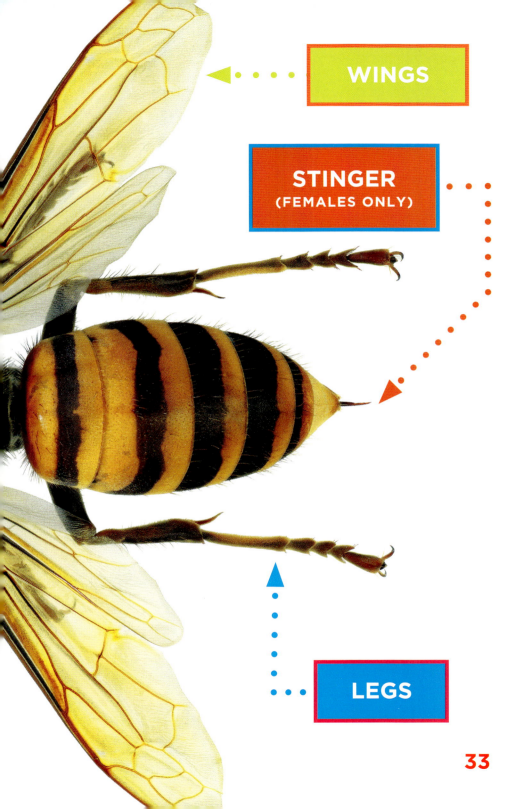

CHAPTER 9

Where They Live and

Asian giant hornets live primarily *(pry-MARE-ih-lee)* in forests in Asia. However, a few nests have been found in parts of the United States.

Each colony builds a large nest in a tree trunk or underground. The nests can be up to 24 inches underground. Giant hornets also build nests in buildings. Their nests look like paper. They build them out of chewed-up wood and spit.

Tree Nest

Underground Nest

Where Asian Giant Hornets Live

From Egg to ADULT

EGG

Queens lay eggs, which hatch in about a week.

LARVA
Workers feed the larva.

PUPA *(PYOO-puh)*
About two weeks after hatching, a larva seals itself into a cocoon *(kuh-KOON)*. While in the cocoon, it grows into an adult.

ADULT
About two weeks later, a hornet becomes an adult. Queen Asian giant hornets live about one year. Workers live from spring to winter.

CHAPTER 10

WATCH OUT
for Hornets!

Ouch! Asian giant hornets have painful stings. They can wipe out an entire honeybee colony in a few hours. These aggressive *(uh-GRES-siv)* bugs attack anything that gets too close to their nests, including people. Their venom can damage a person's organs *(OR-ganz)*. Some people die from giant hornet stings. If stung, people should hurry to the hospital. These dangerous bugs should be left alone!

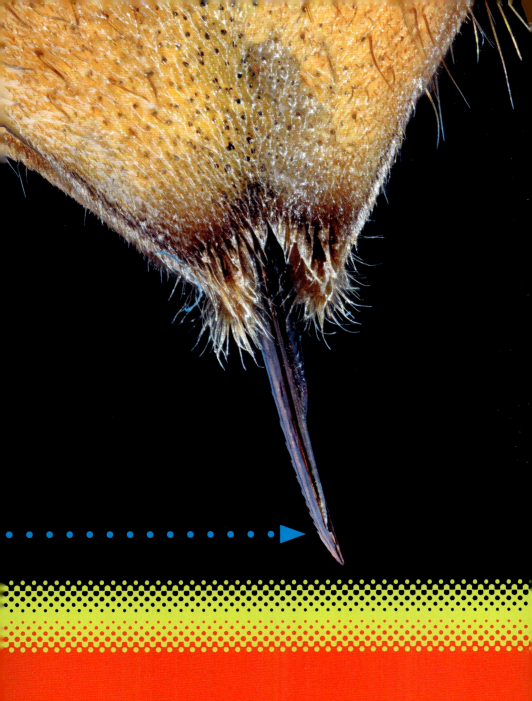

These bugs kill 30 to 50 people in Japan *(juh-PAN)* each year.

By the Numbers

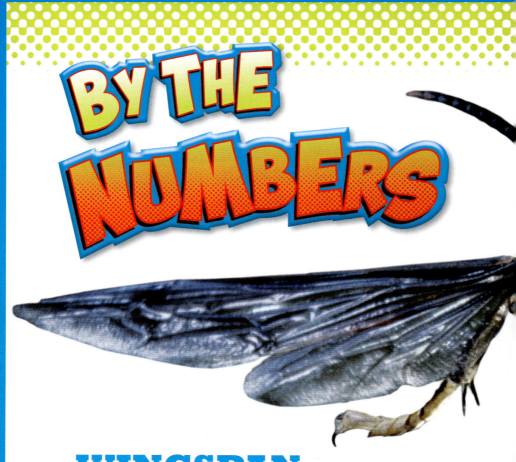

WINGSPAN

1.5 to 3 INCHES

10,000 AVERAGE *(AV-eh-rij)* NUMBER OF EGGS A QUEEN LAYS IN ITS LIFETIME

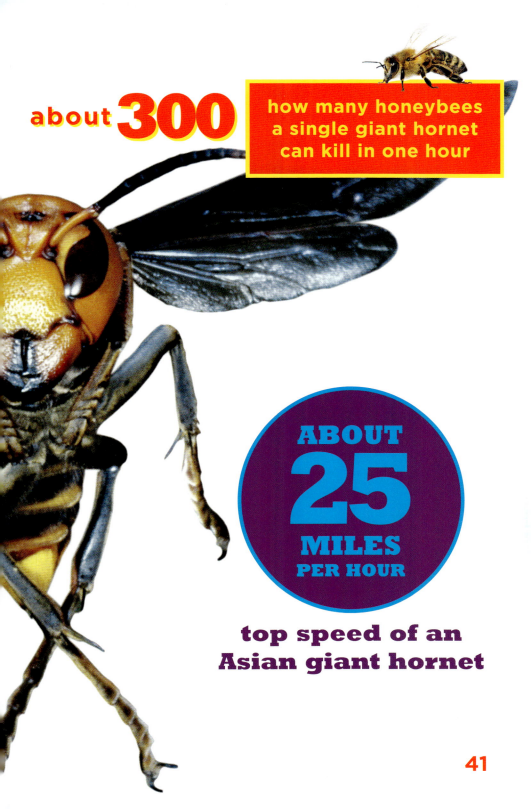

about **300** — how many honeybees a single giant hornet can kill in one hour

ABOUT **25** MILES PER HOUR

top speed of an Asian giant hornet

41

GLOSSARY

abdomen *(AB-duh-min)*—the rear part of an insect's body

aggressive *(uh-GRES-siv)*—showing a readiness to fight, argue, or attack

colony *(KOL-uh-nee)*—a group of animals of the same type living closely together

larva *(LAR-vuh)*—the wormlike form of an animal that hatches from an egg

organ *(OR-gen)*—a structure inside the body made of cells and tissues that performs a specific function

pollen *(POL-len)*—powdery, yellow grains on flowering plants

thorax *(THOR-ax)*—the middle section of an insect's body

venom *(VEN-um)*—a poison made by animals used to kill or injure

Making Difficult Words Easy

Code Reader Books provide codes with "sound keys" to help read difficult words. For example, a word that may be challenging to read is "chameleon," so it might be followed by a code like this: chameleon *(kuh-MEE-lee-un)*.

The codes use phonetic keys for each sound in the word. Knowing the keys can help make reading the codes easier.

Code Reader™ Keys

Long a sound (as in make):
a *(with a silent e)*, **ai**, or **ay**
Examples: break *(brake)*; area *(AIR-ee-uh)*; able *(AY-bul)*

Short a sound (as in cat): **a**
Example: practice *(PRAK-tis)*

Long e sound (as in keep): **ee**
Example: complete *(kum-PLEET)*

Short e sound (as in set): **e** or **eh**
Examples: metric *(MEH-trik)*; bread *(bred)*

Long i sound (as in by):
i *(with a silent e)* or **y**
Examples: might *(mite)*; bicycle *(BY-sih-kul)*

Short i sound (as in sit): **i** or **ih**
Examples: myth *(mith)*; condition *(kun-DIH-shun)*

Long u sound (as in cube): **yoo**
Example: unicorn *(YOO-nih-korn)*

Short u or schwa sound (as in cup):
u or **uh**
Examples: pension *(PEN-shun)*; about *(uh-BOWT)*

Long o sound (as in hope):
o *(with a silent e)*, **oh**, or **o** at the end of a syllable
Examples: molten *(MOLE-ten)*; ocean *(OH-shen)*; nobody *(NO-bah-dee)*

Short o sound (as in top): **o** or **ah**
Examples: posture *(POS-chur)*; bother *(BAH-ther)*

Long oo sound (as in cool): **oo**
Example: school *(skool)*

Short oo sound (as in look): **o͝o**
Examples: wood *(wo͝od)*; could *(ko͝od)*

oy sound (as in boy): **oy**
Example: boisterous *(BOY-stur-us)*

ow sound (as in cow): **ow**
Example: discount *(DIS-kownt)*

aw sound (as in paw): **aw**
Example: faucet *(FAW-sit)*

qu sound (as in quit): **kw**
Example: question *(KWES-chun)*

zh sound (as in garage): **zh**
Example: fission *(FIH-zhun)*

QUESTIONS TO THINK ABOUT

1. If you found a bee hive, what do you think you should do? What is something you should NOT do?

2. What do you think are some ways invasive insects could get to a new area of the world?

3. There are a lot of dangerous insects in the world. If humans had a way to eliminate all the dangerous insects, do you think we should do that? Why or why not?

4. Why do you think the queen bees and queen hornets are important to their colonies?

5. If you were interested in learning more about invasive or dangerous insects, how do you think you could learn more about them?